I0819321

better together*

* This book is best read together, grownup and kid.

a
kids
book
about

a kids book about SUN SAFETY

by Michelle Monaghan

A Kids Book About
Editor Emma Wolf
Head of Design Rick DeLucco
Publisher Jelani Memory

DK
Senior Production Editor Jennifer Murray
Senior Production Controller Louise Minihane
Managing Editor Hazel Eriksson
Publishing Director Mark Searle

This American Edition, 2026
Published in the United States by DK Publishing,
a Division of Penguin Random House LLC
1745 Broadway, 20th Floor, New York, NY 10019

26 27 28 29 10 9 8 7 6 5 4 3 2
002—345282—May/26

First published in Great Britain in 2026 by
Dorling Kindersley Limited, 20 Vauxhall Bridge Road, London SW1V 2SA
A Penguin Random House Company

The authorised representative in the EEA is
Dorling Kindersley Verlag GmbH. Arnulfstr. 124, 80636 Munich, Germany

A CIP catalogue record for this book is available from the British Library

ISBN 978-0-2417-2038-7

Printed and bound in Canada

www.dk.com

akidsco.com

This book was made with Forest Stewardship Council™ certified paper – one small step in DK's commitment to a sustainable future.
Learn more at www.dk.com/uk/information/sustainability

To my husband, Pete, and my
beloved children, Willow and Tommy.
You are the brightest parts of my life.

Intro
for grownups

Attention: Sunny days ahead. Sun protection required! Did you know that 1 in 5 people will get skin cancer in their lifetime? I know this because I was one of them.

I was diagnosed with melanoma in 2005. I beat it, thank goodness, but my diagnosis inspired a deep-dive into all things skin cancer education and prevention. I learned a lot, and I want everyone else to be aware too.

That's why I wrote this book. Because skin cancer prevention is for everyone, not just those with a diagnosis. Most skin cancers are preventable, and this book will help you understand what skin cancer is, how to identify it, and how to take active steps that can lower your risk. Trust me—this sun safety book has got you covered from head to toe.

Hi, my name is MICHELLE!

This is my book all about

SUN SAF

and how to be SUN SAVVY.

FIRST, A LITTLE ABOUT ME.

I grew up in a small town
of 700 people in rural Iowa.

And we were outside all the time.

Each of us kids got 5 dollars
an hour for doing chores
around the farm.

It was awesome!

But this also meant that I was

IN THE SUN ALL THE TIME.

Which sounds fun, but I was never

PROTECTED

from the sun.

(More on that later.)

WHEN I WAS A TEENARGER,

I used something called a tanning bed*.

*Tanning beds are these little pods you lay in that shine bright lights on you and darken your skin.

I thought it made me look cool, but I didn't know how dangerous they were.

HERE'S THE THING:

when I was a kid, there was very little awareness about sun safety.

Unfortunately, I had to learn

THE HARD WAY.

ONE DAY, when I was all grown up, my husband noticed a mole on the back of my leg.

He grew up in Australia, where every kid learns a lot about sun safety.

When he pointed out my mole,
I didn't take him seriously.

I thought it was totally fine.

But I eventually decided to go to
the doctor, and after they
looked at my leg...

they told
me I had
something
called

"mel

anoma".

I had never heard of
melanoma before.

So I didn't know that I had
a type of skin cancer.

That's when I realized it was
REALLY SERIOUS.

I had to get surgery, do recovery,
and life was different after that.

It was time to get

sun
sav

VY!

Here's what I learned:

FIRST,

did you know that our skin is our biggest organ? That's right!

Our skin regenerates over time, meaning you're always getting new layers of skin.

We never know what our new skin will reveal, so it's important to always protect it.

second,

the sun is so powerful.

It emits something called **ultraviolet rays**.

These rays are split into two main types: **UV-A** and **UV-B**.

UV-A causes you to age faster. It can even damage your DNA.

UV-B causes sunburns and contributes most to skin cancer.

THIRD,

did you know the sun is at its most powerful between 10 a.m. and 4 p.m., when its UV rays are the strongest?

And did you know that even when it's cloudy, UV rays can still damage your skin?

I told you,

THE SUN IS

POW

ERFUL.

And I don't want you
to be scared of it!

Life on this planet literally
couldn't exist without the sun.

Plants, animals, and all of
us humans—we need
the sun to survive.

But it's important to get just the right amount.

SO, WHAT CAN YOU DO TO STAY SUN SAFE?

WEAR
SUNSCR

een.

It sounds simple, but it's so important.

Wearing sunscreen keeps your skin safe from the most dangerous parts of the sun when it shines on you.

So, before you go outside, apply sunscreen.

Put it anywhere on your body that will be exposed to the sun. And reapply it every couple of hours.

And make sure your sunscreen is SPF* 30 or higher.

*Your grownup can explain what SPF means!

wear a hat some-times.

Yes, even if you have lots of hair, a hat still protects the top of your head and your face from the sun.

WEAR PROTECTIVE CLOTHING.

When you're at the beach or playing outside, the best way to protect your skin is to cover it up.

And there's one more really important thing:

CHECKS.

THIS IS A SUPER EASY WAY

to make sure your skin is still healthy.

Doing a skin check means looking at any moles or freckles on your skin that have changed or grown over time.

Are they uneven?

Are they asymmetrical, meaning are they shaped strangely?

Definitely take note of any new moles or ones you didn't notice during your last skin check.

AND BE

every

SURE TO

OK

WHERE!

ON TOP OF YOUR HEAD,
BEHIND YOUR EARS.

On your hands and fingernails,
and even between your toes.

Here's the thing—

sun safety every

IS FOR

BODY.

IF YOU HAVE SKIN,

sun safety is for you.

No matter your gender, skin color, or where you live, sun safety is important for

everyone.

While the sun is super powerful,

so
are
you!

You can show your power every
day by making sun-safe choices.

LET'S THRIVE AND SHINE TOGETHER!

Outro for grownups

So, why am I telling you all of this? Because I want to empower you to protect the skin you're in. It's the only one you've got!

I didn't grow up learning about skin cancer or sun safety, but I want to make sure you and the kids in your life do.

Most skin cancer is preventable, which means you can stop it from ever happening to you.

I love being outside and enjoying fun in the sun, and you can too! But before you head out on your next adventure, here's a simple and sun-savvy checklist to walk through with your family:

- Are you wearing sunscreen?
- Do you have protective clothing on, like a hat?
- Now, are you ready to have a good time!?

If you answered yes to all three, shine on! You're officially sun savvy!

About The Author

My name is Michelle Monaghan (she/her), and I'm an actor, skin cancer survivor, and skin cancer prevention advocate. I've worked in the film and television industry since the early 2000s and have appeared in numerous films and television series.

In 2005, I was diagnosed with melanoma, the most serious type of skin cancer. This book is about my cancer journey, and how it inspired me to educate myself and others about skin cancer prevention and all the ways that we can stay safe in the sun.

I'm proud to spread awareness and empower you to protect yourself from the most common, yet most preventable, form of cancer. I hope you enjoy this book and continue to shine on!